DISCOVERY BOOKS

BIG CATS

Editor Jessica Cohn
Publishing Director Chester Fisher
Client Service Manager Santosh Vasudevan
Project Manager Shekhar Kapur
Creative Director Simmi Sikka
Designer Joita Das and Shilpi Sarkar
Picture Researcher Kamal Kumar

10 9 8 7 6 5 4 3 2 1

ISBN-10: 0-545-17494-5
ISBN-13: 978-0-545-17494-7

Printed in China

Picture Credits

Cover Images:
Front Cover: Q2AMedia Artwork
Back Cover: ltterry: Istockphoto
Title Page: Keith Levit: Shutterstock
Imprint Page: Jan Daly: Shutterstock
Half Title: Flickr
Content Page: Christopher P. Grant: Shutterstock, 33t Alan and Sandy Carey: Gettyimages, Joshua Haviv: Shutterstock.

6tl Spingold Graphics: Istockphoto. 6bl Keith Levit: Shutterstock. 6br Johanna Goodyear: Istockphoto. 6-7m Maxim Kazitov: Shutterstock. 7tr diane: Istockphoto. 10tl JJMaree: Istockphoto. 10br Wild Wing Carving: Istockphoto. 11 Johan Swanepoel: Shutterstock. 12-13 Beat Glauser: Shutterstock. 13t Greg Johnson: Shutterstock. 14l Istockphoto.

14rb stephenmeese: Istockphoto, Marina Cano Trueba: Shutterstock. 15 Christopher P. Grant: Shutterstock. 16-17 Kateryna Potrokhova: Shutterstock. 16tr Graça Victoria: Dreamstime. 17tr Marina Cano Trueba: Shutterstock. 18l Cindy Haggerty: Shutterstock. 18r Chin Kit Sen: Shutterstock. 19t jeff51: Istockphoto. 19b Marbo: Istockphoto. 20t M. Robbemont: Shutterstock. 20b Shutterstock. 21t EcoPrint: Shutterstock. 22b GomezDavid: Istockphoto. 22-23t Shutterstock. 22-23b Vasiliy Koval: Shutterstock. 24 Elena Sherengovskaya: Shutterstock. 26 EcoPrint: Shutterstock. 26-27 Shutterstock. 27 AfriPics.com: Alamy. 28 Vasiliy Koval: Shutterstock. 29 Javarman: 123rf. 30t angelofthemaya.com. 30b World Pictures: Alamy. 30-31 Susan E. Degginger: Alamy. 32-33t Alan and Sandy Carey: Gettyimages. 32-33b ltterry: Istockphoto. 33t photobar: Shutterstock. 33b Steffen Foerster Photography: Shutterstock. 34 Impalastock: Istockphoto.

34-35 Arco Images GmbH: Alamy. 35t Flickr. 36 Jan Daly: Shutterstock. 36-37 Joshua Haviv: Shutterstock. 37t JJMaree: Istockphoto, Geoffrey Kuchera: Shutterstock. 38 Shutterstock. 38-39 Jan Daly/Shutterstock. 39t Cay-Uwe: Istockphoto. 40 Calvin Lee: Shutterstock. 40-41 LambertDavid: Istockphoto. 42-43 Chris Fourie: Dreamstime. 42b Graca Victoria: Shutterstock. 43 Shutterstock. 44-45 Kateryna Potrokhova: Shutterstock. 44tr angelofthemaya.com. 45tr diane: Istockphoto. 46 Vasiliy Koval: Shutterstock. 47tr photobar: Shutterstock.

DISCOVERY BOOKS

BIG CATS

Sujatha Menon

Contents

Know Your Cats

Big cats have sharp teeth that help them tear meat into small pieces.

Big cats are not very different from your pet cat—they all belong to the same family. Big cats are really oversized house cats. They behave the same way as pet cats. Just watch your cat closely and you notice the similarities.

A cat's life

Big cats love meat. In fact, tigers are even known to hunt for fish. Big cats have excellent vision and a good sense of hearing. They also have sharp claws and teeth, all of which are important tools for a predator. Most cats have a **flexible** spine, a round head, and a furry coat. Big cats are muscular and have powerful jaws. They can overcome even the largest prey with their strength.

*Its size and strength has made the lion the top **predator** of the savannas. Its majestic look earned this big cat the nickname "king of the jungle."*

Tigers love water. In fact, tigers will chase prey into a stream because they find it easy to hunt in water.

Pet cats are much smaller and milder than their wild cousins.

Feline facts

Total number of cat species: 36

Family: Felidae

True big cats: Tiger, lion, jaguar, and leopard

Other large cats: Cheetah, snow leopard, clouded leopard, and puma

Medium-sized cats: Lynx, ocelot, caracal, bobcat and serval

Roar for a big cat!

There are many similarities between a pet cat and a big cat, but there are also differences. So, how do you identify a big cat? The size helps you tell a big cat and a pet cat apart, but did you know that all large cats are not big cats? Only four species are considered to be big cats. They are tigers, lions, leopards, and jaguars. These cats can roar!

▲ *The cheetah can't roar. Therefore, it is not a true big cat. However, it has all the other features of a big cat.*

The hyoid bone!

A unique feature of a true big cat is its ability to roar. All cats have a **hyoid** in the mouth. This structure connects the tongue to the roof of the mouth. In small cats, the hyoid is hardened into a bone. However, in big cats this structure is flexible and helps them produce a loud roar.

Prehistoric Cats

Like all creatures on Earth, big cats have **ancestors**. Cats have been around for more than 30 million years. Modern big cats are believed to have **evolved** from a common ancestor about 2 to 3 million years ago.

Proailurus

The *Proailurus* (pro-ay-lyou-rus) was the earliest known ancestor of cats. The name means "old cat." And it really was very old. This cat is believed to have lived about 30 million years ago. It probably was the first cat to ever roam our planet. The *Proailurus* was not very big. It was the size of a bobcat. It had more teeth than its descendants.

▼ A recreation from the fossil of the Proailurus, the ancestor of all cats.

Sabre-toothed cats

The sabre-toothed cats are the best-known prehistoric cats. These cats had very long upper **canines**. Sabre-toothed cats used these teeth like a knife. The *Smilodon* and the scimitar cat were the most famous of the sabre-toothed cats.

▲ This ferocious cat is Smilodon. Its fossil records show its teeth grew to about 7 in. (17 cm) in length!

Proailurus facts

Lived: *about 30 million years ago*

Size: *just a little larger than a pet cat*

Weighed: *20 lbs. (9 kg)*

Was followed by: *Pseudaelurus (direct ancestor of big cats)*

Another descendant: *Machairodus (ancestor of Smilodon)*

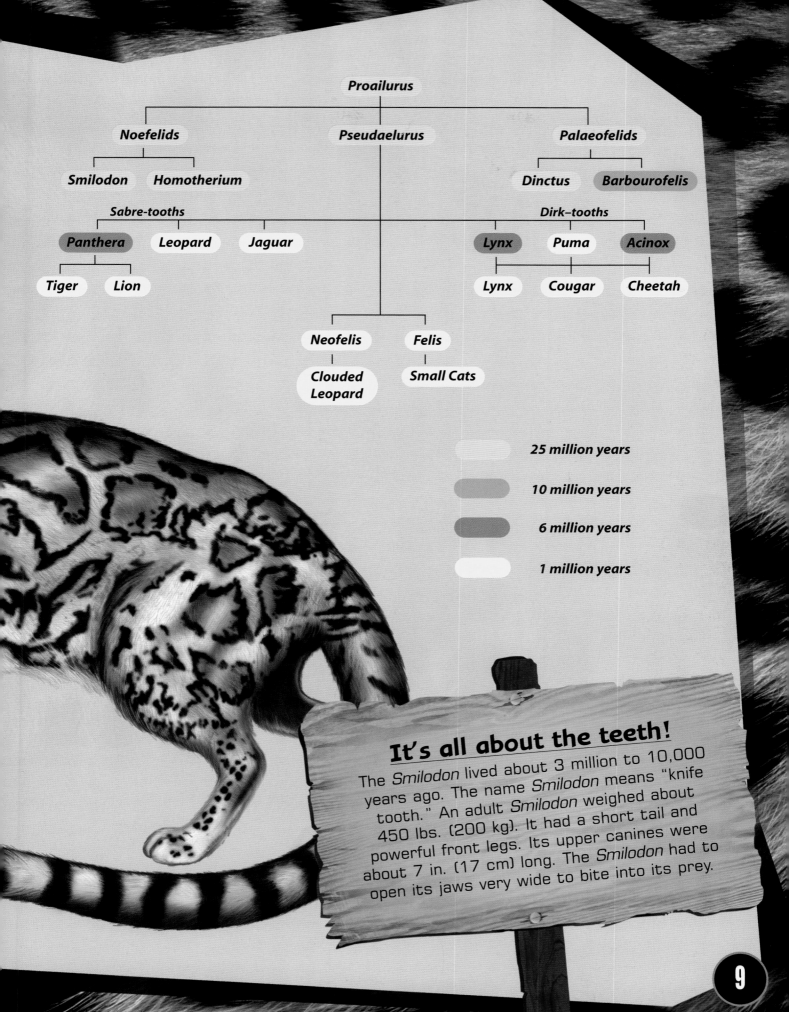

Proailurus

Noefelids — Pseudaelurus — Palaeofelids

Smilodon — Homotherium — Dinctus — Barbourofelis

Sabre-tooths — Dirk-tooths

Panthera — Leopard — Jaguar — Lynx — Puma — Acinox

Tiger — Lion — Lynx — Cougar — Cheetah

Neofelis — Felis

Clouded Leopard — Small Cats

25 million years

10 million years

6 million years

1 million years

It's all about the teeth!

The *Smilodon* lived about 3 million to 10,000 years ago. The name *Smilodon* means "knife tooth." An adult *Smilodon* weighed about 450 lbs. (200 kg). It had a short tail and powerful front legs. Its upper canines were about 7 in. (17 cm) long. The *Smilodon* had to open its jaws very wide to bite into its prey.

Deadly Teeth

Teeth are important to all of us. We wouldn't be able to bite or chew our food without them. Big cats must hunt for their meals. Their teeth, are designed for grasping prey and tearing flesh. They are the felines' most important tools.

◀ *Unlike dogs, cats do not **gnaw** on bones. This keeps their teeth from breaking.*

▼ *A big cat's **incisors** are so sharp they can cut through the tough skin of a cape buffalo.*

Teething facts

Big cats usually have about 30 teeth—all designed to slice flesh.

Canines: 4

Incisors: 12

Premolars: 8

Molars: 2

Carnassials: 4

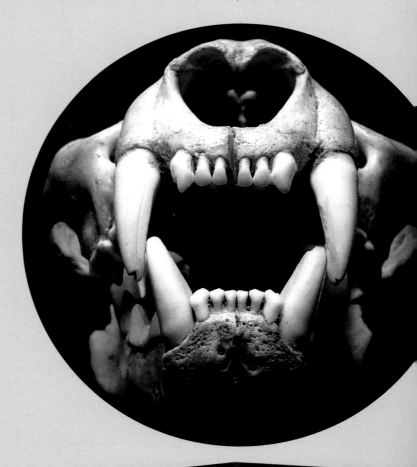

Killer canines

Those huge canines on this skull help cats bite and kill their prey. The canines of big cats look and function like small daggers. When a cat catches an animal, it drives its canine teeth into the victim.

Mealtime

Once the prey is dead, the cat settles down to gulp its meal because they can't chew. Cats use their powerful shearing teeth, called **carnassials**, to cut meat into small pieces that are easy to swallow. Small, sharp incisor teeth arranged between the canines in the front of its mouth help the cat grasp its food and scrape meat off the bones.

▶ *The carnassials of a big cat can shear through flesh the same way scissors cut through paper.*

Tooth troubles

The *Smilodon* had long sawlike canine teeth in the upper jaw. These teeth were so weak they broke if the cat bit into its prey. Therefore, the *Smilodon* used its short lower canines to kill its prey. It then closed its jaws so the **serrated** edges would **shear** through the prey's skin like a saw.

Paws and Claws

Other than teeth, big cats also have claws to help them. A cat's claws are sharp and curved, making it impossible for its victim to escape. If attacked, cats can deliver a painful, and even **fatal**, wound with their claws.

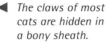

◀ *The claws of most cats are hidden in a bony sheath.*

▲ *RETRACTED*

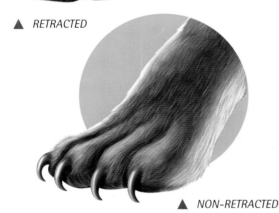

▲ *NON-RETRACTED*

Hidden claws

If you look closely at the paws of your pet cat, you may or may not see its claws, because they are simply hidden. All cats, except cheetahs, have **retractable** claws that are drawn into their paws when not in use. This prevents the cat from hurting itself while grooming. The **menacing** claws come out only when the cat pounces or defends itself.

Tip-toed

Cats are digitigrades, meaning they walk on their toes. It is believed that cats once walked on their entire paw. However, over millions of years, the backs of their feet slowly raised until they began to walk on their toes. This feature helps cats run faster—a great advantage when chasing animals, such as antelope.

Paw trail

Cats use their paws to touch and feel objects and for washing and grooming their fur. The padded undersides help them move silently and run quickly. The front paws have five claws. The fifth claw at the back of each front paw is called a *dewclaw* and is believed to have been the cat's heel at one time. The hind paws have four claws.

▲ Their soft pads help cats to move quietly.

◄ Cats use their dewclaws to hold prey and stay balanced while climbing.

Claw facts

Claws are used:

- To grasp prey
- For cleaning the fur
- For marking their territory by scratching trees
- For climbing trees and ledges. Big cats, such as leopards and jaguars, climb trees a lot, and claws help them grip tree bark. Claws also help prevent some cats, such as the snow leopard, from slipping on the ice.
- In defense. Big cats protect themselves by swiping at their enemies with their claws.

Cat Vision

It's common knowledge that cats see well in the dark. This is probably why most cats hunt better at night.

Mirror in the eyes

Most big cats prefer to hunt between sunset and sunrise. The eyes of big cats are designed for seeing in dim light. Try this experiment with the help of an adult. Hold a mirror against sunlight and focus the reflected light onto a wall or floor. You'll see the reflection of a bright spot of light. Cat eyes have a structure that reflects light just like the mirror in order to help them see better in dim conditions.

▲ *During the day, the pupils become smaller to block bright light. The mirrorlike feature of the eyes is the reason for poor vision during the day.*

Vision facts

A big cat:

- *Can detect movements that are too fast for humans to see*
- *Can't see slow movements*
- *Can see clearly in dim light due to a mirrorlike structure in the eye called* **tapetum lucidum**
- *Can't see very well during the day or in total darkness*
- *Can judge distances accurately*
- *Can't make out colors very well*

The picture on the top right is that of a tiger's eyes in normal light, while the picture on the bottom was taken in the dark. In dim light, the pupils widen to absorb as much light as possible. The reflected light makes the eyes appear as if they glow in the dark. ▶

Looking forward

The eyes of big cats, like those of all predators, are located at the front of the face. This helps the cat to focus both eyes on one object. Big cats are excellent judges of distance. This is very important because most cats (except the cheetah) approach their prey silently and get as close as possible before pouncing.

◄ *During the day, the pupils become smaller to block bright light. The mirrorlike feature of the eyes is the reason for poor vision during the day.*

Colorblind?

It is believed that the eyes of big cats are designed to help them judge distances and see in the dark, not to identify color. Until recently, it was thought that cats were completely colorblind. However, it is now known that cats are able to identify some colors such as blue, green, and yellow, along with shades of gray.

Other Senses

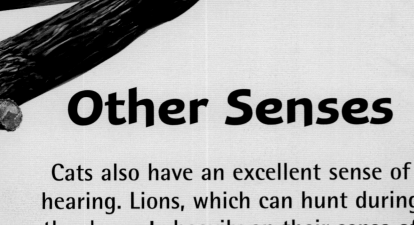

Cats also have an excellent sense of hearing. Lions, which can hunt during the day, **rely** heavily on their sense of hearing to locate prey. Cats can also **detect** different kinds of smells, although they are not as good as dogs.

▲ Cats are able to hear over a very wide range of frequencies, almost five times better than human hearing.

Listening

The short, cup-shaped ears of a big cat are extremely sensitive. The cat can pick up the sound of a twig breaking. It is believed that most big cats can tell the difference between rustling leaves and the sound of an animal brushing past a bush.

Incredible senses

- *Big cats can distinguish between the scents of male and female cats.*
- *Big cats can tell whether a particular scent belongs to an animal from the same area or from a stranger.*
- *Whiskers indicate the mood of a big cat. The whiskers of a calm big cat are turned down, while those of an aggressive cat are stiff.*
- *Cats can't detect sweetness, but they are extremely sensitive to the tiniest difference in the taste of the water they drink.*

Just a touch

The whiskers of a cat are not for decoration. They are very important to a cat's movements and help the animal find its way in the dark. The whiskers are so sensitive that they can detect even the slightest change in wind direction, letting the cat know that there is an **obstacle** nearby. You might have seen a cat stick its head into narrow openings. This is because the whiskers help the cat judge whether it can fit into the space.

▲ *The cat's whiskers are extremely sensitive and can register very small changes in air pressure, enabling them to avoid objects while moving around in the dark.*

Scent of a cat

Why does a tiger often open its mouth wide and hang its tongue out? To smell! Big cats such as tigers and lions have two tiny openings called a *Jacobson's organ* on the roof of the mouth. By opening their mouths wide, these cats allow the scent to be identified when it enters the brain.

Fur and Patterns

One of the easiest ways to tell big cats from one another is by looking at their fur and the patterns on them. All big cats have coats that are suited to the environment in which they live.

Warm Coats

Big cats that live in cold regions have long, thick fur all over the body, which protects these animals from the cold. Some large cats, such as snow leopards, even have fur on the bottom of their paws that helps keep the cats warm and prevents their feet from sinking into the snow. The snow leopard also has long, woolly fur on its belly for protecting the part of its body that is closest to the ground. Cats such as lions and cheetahs have short fur because they live in much warmer climates.

▲ *Note the difference in **texture** and color of the fur of the Siberian tiger (above) and the Royal Bengal tiger (right). They live in very different environments.*

Designed to hide

The coats of big cats come in various colors and patterns, which also change according to the habitat. For example, the lion, which lives in the open savanna, has a sandy brown coat that helps it blend in with its surroundings. The tiger's striped coat provides excellent camouflage in thick jungles, while the leopard's golden yellow, spotted coat makes it almost invisible among the tall grass of the savanna or up on tree branches.

Coat facts

- *Tiger: Reddish-orange coat with black or dark brown stripes*
- *Lion: Sandy brown coats. Males have a dark brown mane on the head*
- *Leopard: Golden yellow base color with dark brown or black **rosettes** (broken circles)*
- *Jaguar: Brownish-yellow coat with dark rosettes. Unlike the spots of a leopard, jaguar's rosettes have small dots inside some of them*
- *Cheetah: Yellow coat with black or brown dots*

The sandy brown coat of the lioness matches the color of the tall grass, making it difficult to be seen either by its prey or its enemy.

▼ This lion is grooming itself. A rough tongue helps it clean and comb its fur.

Licking clean

Cats are very fussy about their coats. Even pet cats spend hours licking their coats clean, and big cats are no different. All cats have tiny hooklike structures called *papillae* on their tongues. These are used to clean their fur. They also use their claws to comb out parasites and dead skin.

Caring for Cubs

Big cats, like almost all mammals, give birth to live young. A big cat's young one is called a *cub*. The mother takes care of the cubs, but the father is not involved in cub-rearing.

The mother usually carries a cub in her mouth, holding it carefully by its neck.

Helpless cubs

Cubs are born blind and are totally dependent on their mother. The mother hides her cubs in a safe place and stays with them until they are able to walk around. The cubs live on their mother's milk for the first six months. Once the cubs start eating meat, the mother takes them on hunting trips.

When the cubs are about a year old, they **accompany** their mother on a hunt and learn by **mimicking** her.

The hyena is the biggest enemy of lion cubs. A group of hyenas can distract the adult lions while the others steal the cubs.

Cubs in danger

From the moment they are born, cubs need to be protected from predators. The mother moves them from one hiding place to another to keep them safe. Lionesses fiercely defend their cubs against **intruders** and often succeed in driving enemies away. The males will defend an entire pride. Lions are especially ferocious when defending their young from foes such as hyenas. Male tigers are also known to keep watch over their young, while cheetahs and leopards put their cubs up in trees to protect them.

Life span in the wild

Tigers: live for up to 15 years

Lions: live for 10-12 years

Jaguars: live for about 12 years

Leopards: live up to 17 years

Cheetahs: live up to 12 years

Staying together

Male lion cubs stay with their **pride** only until they are about two years old, after which they are either driven out or leave the group on their own. A group of male lions sometimes forms a bachelor pride. Each one of them tries to take over another pride that has lionesses. When a young male takes over a pride, he kills all the cubs in that pride.

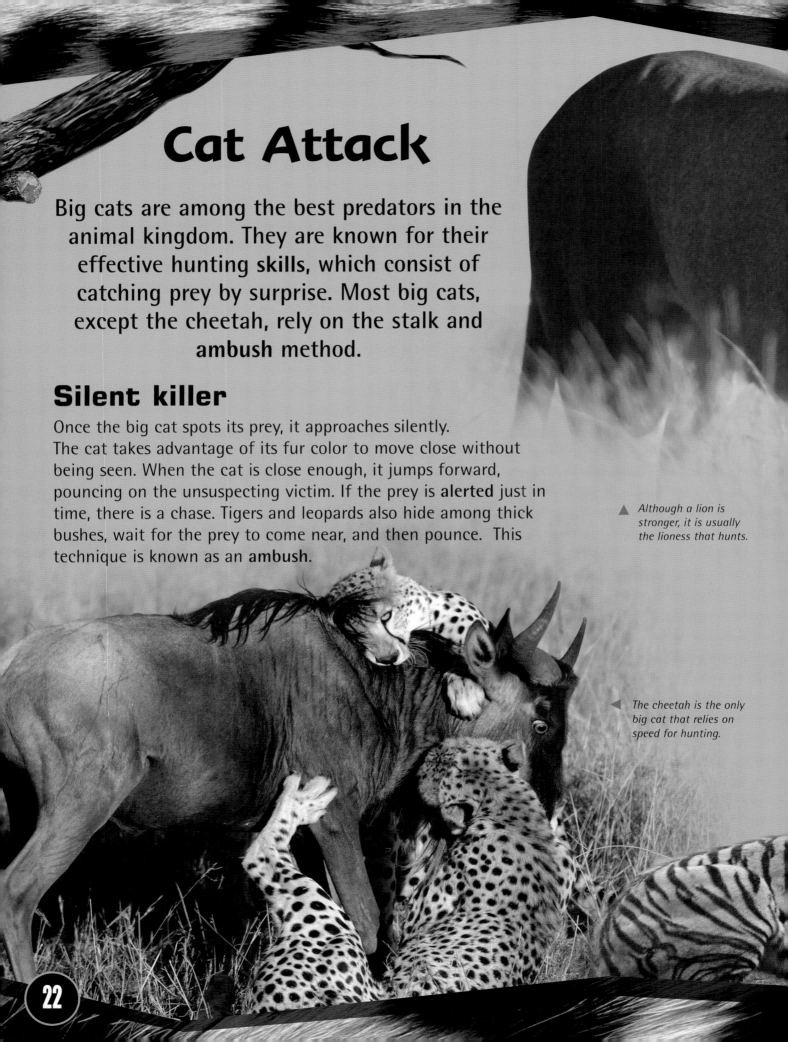

Cat Attack

Big cats are among the best predators in the animal kingdom. They are known for their effective hunting **skills**, which consist of catching prey by surprise. Most big cats, except the cheetah, rely on the stalk and **ambush** method.

Silent killer

Once the big cat spots its prey, it approaches silently. The cat takes advantage of its fur color to move close without being seen. When the cat is close enough, it jumps forward, pouncing on the unsuspecting victim. If the prey is **alerted** just in time, there is a chase. Tigers and leopards also hide among thick bushes, wait for the prey to come near, and then pounce. This technique is known as an **ambush**.

Although a lion is stronger, it is usually the lioness that hunts.

The cheetah is the only big cat that relies on speed for hunting.

How prey react

Many prey animals respond differently to a cat attack:

- *Elephants: Often injure cats with their tusks or trample them. A herd of elephants surround their young to defend them.*
- *Zebras: The herd leader alerts the rest of the herd to the danger. He then kicks out at the cat and tries to distract it, giving the herd time to get away.*
- *Wildebeest: These animals are known to break out into a stampede.*

Defending their own

Big cats might be fierce hunters, but even they have to defend themselves against various dangers. Female big cats are very aggressive when defending their cubs and their kills from animals such as hyenas. All big cats are highly **territorial**—they claim a certain area as their own and defend it. This can lead to fights between members of the same species.

▼ *When an intruder refuses to leave the territory of a big cat, there is a fight between them.*

Marking territory

All big cats have a certain territory that includes hunting grounds, dens, and even water holes that they don't like to share. They mark these territories so no other cat invades their space by spraying urine, scratching trees, or rubbing their cheeks against rocks, trees, or other objects. Intruding cats usually leave the area once they smell or see the signs.

Tiger

Tigers are the largest of the big cats. The biggest tigers are larger and heavier than even male lions. Tigers are highly territorial and, like most big cats, prefer to live and hunt alone. Tigers and jaguars are the only big cats that like to swim.

Fatal leap

Most tigers have an orange coat with black or brown vertical stripes. This unusual coloring helps the tiger hide in the thick jungles where it lives. The tiger uses its camouflage to avoid being seen while stalking its prey. When it is close enough, the tiger leaps through the air and pounces. The sheer weight of this large cat is enough to knock its prey down in order to deliver the **fatal** bite.

▼ *The powerful tiger is a good swimmer and is known to swim distances of 18 mi. (29 km) at a time!*

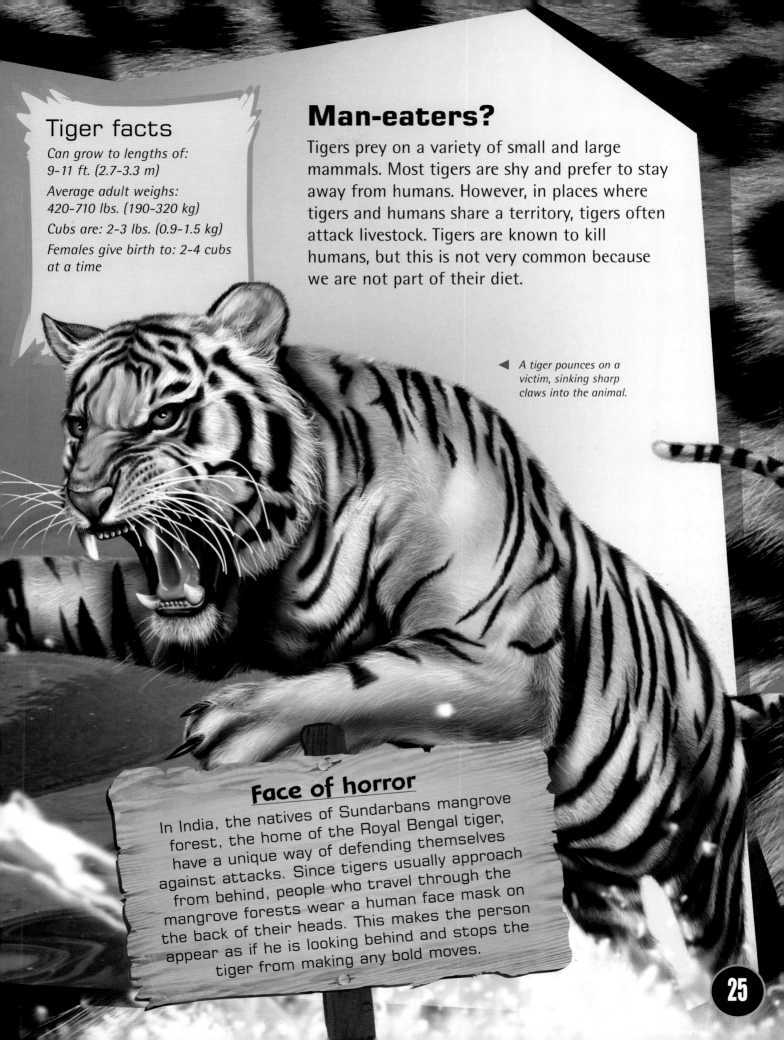

Tiger facts

Can grow to lengths of:
9-11 ft. (2.7-3.3 m)

Average adult weighs:
420-710 lbs. (190-320 kg)

Cubs are: 2-3 lbs. (0.9-1.5 kg)

Females give birth to: 2-4 cubs
at a time

Man-eaters?

Tigers prey on a variety of small and large mammals. Most tigers are shy and prefer to stay away from humans. However, in places where tigers and humans share a territory, tigers often attack livestock. Tigers are known to kill humans, but this is not very common because we are not part of their diet.

◄ *A tiger pounces on a victim, sinking sharp claws into the animal.*

Face of horror

In India, the natives of Sundarbans mangrove forest, the home of the Royal Bengal tiger, have a unique way of defending themselves against attacks. Since tigers usually approach from behind, people who travel through the mangrove forests wear a human face mask on the back of their heads. This makes the person appear as if he is looking behind and stops the tiger from making any bold moves.

Lion

The lion is the most majestic of all big cats. It is strong and beautiful, and often seen as a symbol of royalty. Lions were once found throughout Africa and most parts of Western Europe and Asia. Today, they are found only in Central Africa and the Gir Forest in India.

For the pride's sake!

Lions are the only big cats that live in a large family. A group of lions is a pride, and it consists of 10 to 40 individuals. The larger male members are responsible for the protection of the pride. The females in a pride are usually related to one another. Female cubs continue to live in their mother's pride, while male cubs are either driven out or leave on their own when they are about three years old.

The young males are driven out by the head of the pride.

Leonine facts

Can grow to lengths of: 8 ft. (2.5 m) excluding tail

Average adult weighs: 330-550 lbs. (150-250 kg)

Cubs are: 3 lbs. (1.5 kg) at birth

Females give birth to: 1-4 cubs at a time

On the hunt

Lionesses do most of the hunting in a pride. Two or more lionesses hunt together, stalking their prey. However, females do not have enough strength to take down large animals such as wild buffalo. In such cases, they often chase the prey toward the males.

Lionesses do most of the hunting for the pride.

Test of courage

In many parts of the world, killing a lion was considered the ultimate test of courage. This tradition was particularly popular among the Maasai warriors of Kenya. This tribe encouraged its youth to prove their manhood by killing a lion by himself. This has, however, been banned in recent years to protect the lions.

Leopard

Leopards are one of the true big cats. These cats are easily identified by the black ringlike markings on their coat. Unlike those of the jaguar, the leopard's rings do not have spots inside them.

Hard to spot

It is very difficult to see a leopard because they are very shy and come out into the open only at night. During the day, these big cats lie around in trees. It is very difficult to spot a leopard hiding among tree branches. The peculiar markings and light, tan-colored coat provide leopards with excellent camouflage in a wide range of habitats, from open grasslands to thick jungles.

◄ Leopards have massive skulls and very powerful jaw muscles to help them capture prey much bigger than themselves.

Leopard facts

Can grow to lengths of: $6\frac{1}{2}$ ft. (2 m)

Average adult weighs: 60-200 lbs. (30-90 kg)

Cubs are: $1\frac{1}{2}$ lbs. (0.7-1 kg) at birth

Females give birth to: 1-4 cubs at a time

Tree lover

Leopards are very powerful climbers. The strong shoulder and chest muscles of leopards allow these cats to drag prey three times their size high up into the trees. They are known to haul young giraffes onto branches more than 20 ft. (6 m) above the ground and even stalk monkeys in trees.

▶ *Leopards usually drag their prey up tree branches so they are not bothered by hyenas and lions and can therefore eat in peace.*

A hardy life

Leopards eat almost anything, including antelope, giraffes, monkeys, and jackals. Leopards that live near human populations also prey on domestic animals, such as cattle and sheep. These cats can go without water for several days. They obtain the necessary fluids from their prey. This is probably why leopards are able to live in a wide range of habitats and conditions.

Jaguar

Ancient people of Central and South America understood the power of the jaguar. This big cat was worshipped by ancient Mayans, who attributed supernatural powers to them. They believed that the jaguar could communicate between the living and the dead.

There were several jaguar gods in Mayan mythology. Since jaguars are nocturnal, these Mayan gods belonged to the Underworld.

The most powerful

In proportion to its size, the jaguar is considered to be the most powerful of all big cats. It looks similar to the leopard but is heavier and more muscular. The jaguar has short, stocky limbs that help it climb trees. The golden yellow coat has ringlike markings similar to those of the leopard. A jaguar's rosettes have spots in the center.

Jaguars follow footprints to locate their prey. Once the prey is found, the cat gets closer and pounces. If the prey tries to escape by swimming away, the jaguar will leap into the water in pursuit.

Splashing in

Jaguars, like tigers, love to spend time in water, prefering to live near streams and rivers. They are strong swimmers and even hunt while swimming. It is said that a jaguar once killed a cow on the bank of a river and swam more than 2,600 ft. (700 m) across while dragging its prey!

White lions range from snow-white to blond in color. Cubs are usually born white. They turn yellowish-white to blond as they grow.

Born white

Like leopards and jaguars, some tigers and lions also vary in color. However, instead of black, they are usually born white. This condition is caused by a **recessive gene** found in Bengal and Amur tigers and the lions of Timbavati, near Kruger National Park in South Africa. Two animals carrying this gene sometimes produce a white tiger or lion. This is very rare in the wild. Most white lions and tigers are specially bred in zoos.

Other color variations

- **Golden tabby:** *tiger with white coat and gold patches. The fur of tabbies is much softer than that of the normal tigers.*
- **Black tigers:** *melanistic tigers are rarer than black panthers. The dark stripes on these tigers are extremely wide, covering most of the orange color. This makes these cats appear dark in color.*
- **Maltese tigers:** *tigers with a bluish coat and dark gray stripes. People are believed to have seen these tigers in the Fujian Province in China. However, the reports have not been confirmed.*
- **White panthers:** *leopards or jaguars with white to cream-colored coats with faint rosettes.*

A white tiger and a golden tabby in a zoo. These cats are rarely found in the wild.

Unusual Cats

A cat that is half-lion and half-tiger might sound impossible, but it's true. Ligers and other big cat hybrids might be rare, but they do exist in this world.

Crossbreeds

You get different traits from each of your parents. Much the same thing happens when different types of cats are crossbred. The young cats have characteristics of both the mother and the father. A liger, for example, is born to a male lion and a female tiger.

◄ All ligers are born in captivity.

Other hybrids

Ligers and tigons are not the only hybrids. Lions and tigers can mate with other species, such as leopards and jaguars, to produce unusual cats. A jaglion is the young cub of a lioness and a male jaguar. A male jaguar and a female leopard can create a jagulep, while a leopon is the result of a male leopard and a lioness.

Ligers and tigons

A liger looks like a giant lion with faded stripes. Some ligers even have manes. All ligers love to swim. Tigons are born to a lioness and a male tiger. Tigons don't grow as big as ligers. Neither ligers nor tigons are common in the wild because lions and tigers live in different habitats. These hybrids usually occur in zoos and preserves where the enclosures of lions and tigers are close to each other.

Lioness + Male Jaguar → Jaglion

Male Jaguar + Female Leopard → Jagulep

Male Leopard + Lioness → Leopon

Male lion + Female Tiger → Liger

Lioness + Male Tiger → Tigons

Larger than all

A liger named Hercules is the largest of its kind in the world. This liger is housed in Jungle Island, an animal theme park in Miami, Florida. It is about 10 ft. (3 m) long and weighs more than 900 lbs. (400 kg).

Big Cats in Danger

Big cats are at the top of the food chain—they don't have any natural enemies. Even so, most big cats are on the brink of being wiped off the face of Earth, and we have only ourselves to blame for it.

Silent killer

Humans are the biggest enemies of big cats. Until a few decades ago, big cats were plentiful around the world. Today many big cats can be seen only in zoos, wildlife parks, and on television. In fact, there are no more big cats in Europe. One of the main causes is the destruction of forests and other natural habitats of big cats. People clear forests and grasslands so they can build houses and use the land for farming.

▼ *Sensitive tourists can help keep the big cats alive.*

Killing for profit

Apart from destroying the cats' homes, people also kill big cats for their soft fur, teeth, and bones. In some countries, the bones of big cats are considered to have healing properties and are used to make medicines. Teeth and bones are also used to make jewelery. Some people even hunt big cats for sport! The result is that the number of big cats in the wild is going down.

► *The soft furry coats of big cats are used as decorative bags.*

Endangered Cats

Bengal tiger: 2,000-3,000

Indo-Chinese tiger: 1,200

Sumatran tiger: 400-500

Siberian tiger: 400-500

South China tiger: about 59 (all in captivity)

Asiatic lion: 350

Amur leopard: about 50

South Arabian leopard: below 100

North African leopard: below 250

▲ *It can be dangerous for big cats if they trust humans too much.*

Save the cats

Today, many people have realized the importance of preserving big cats. Several organizations have been established to protect these precious animals. Zoos are focusing on breeding big cats in a healthy manner. Many countries have set aside forests and grasslands as *reserves* for big cats. These areas are protected, and people are not allowed to cut trees or live in these areas. The hunting of big cats has also been banned.

Facts and Records

- The Siberian tiger is the largest cat in the world. An adult Siberian tiger can weigh as much as 700 lbs. (317.5 kg)!

- The stripes on individual tigers are never the same. Like human fingerprints, stripes are used to tell one tiger from another.

- The jaws of a cheetah are weak, so it kills its prey by grasping its throat until it suffocates.

- A lion's roar can be heard from 5 mi. (8 km) away.

- A lion usually lives up to 13 years. Nero, the longest known living lion, survived up to 29 years in captivity.

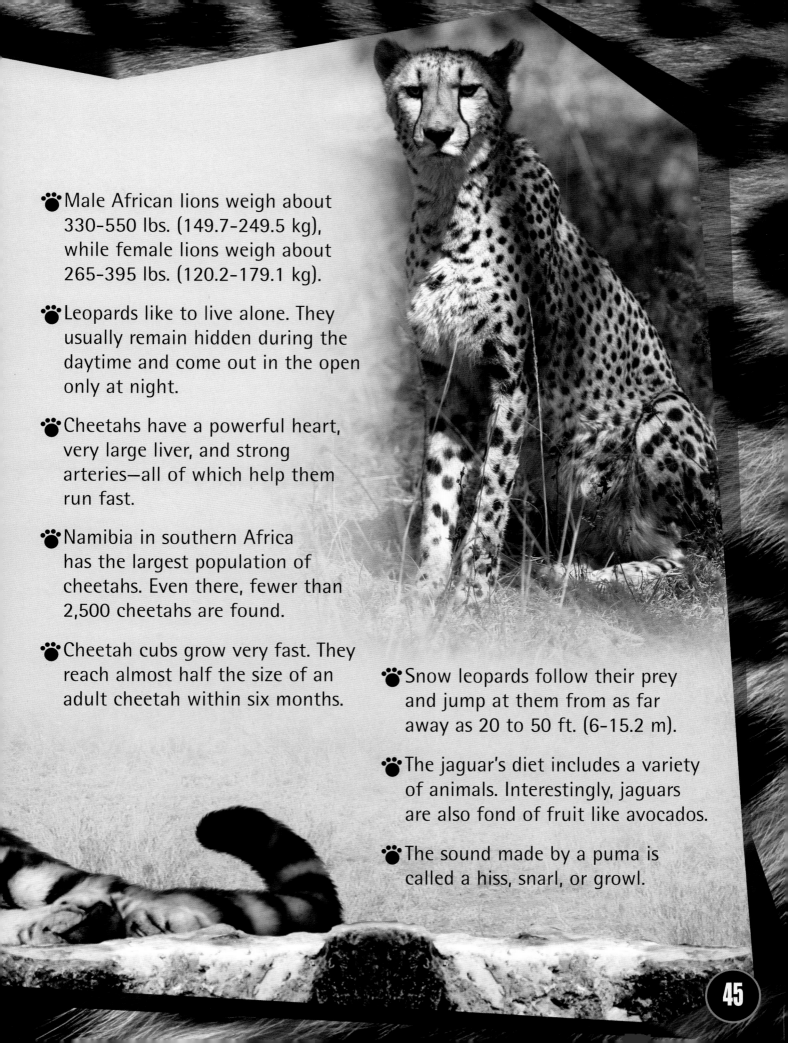

- Male African lions weigh about 330-550 lbs. (149.7-249.5 kg), while female lions weigh about 265-395 lbs. (120.2-179.1 kg).

- Leopards like to live alone. They usually remain hidden during the daytime and come out in the open only at night.

- Cheetahs have a powerful heart, very large liver, and strong arteries—all of which help them run fast.

- Namibia in southern Africa has the largest population of cheetahs. Even there, fewer than 2,500 cheetahs are found.

- Cheetah cubs grow very fast. They reach almost half the size of an adult cheetah within six months.

- Snow leopards follow their prey and jump at them from as far away as 20 to 50 ft. (6-15.2 m).

- The jaguar's diet includes a variety of animals. Interestingly, jaguars are also fond of fruit like avocados.

- The sound made by a puma is called a hiss, snarl, or growl.

Glossary

Accompany Go along with

Alert To warn of danger

Ambush To hide and then attack prey suddenly

Ancestor A person from whom one is descended

Breed To produce a young one with a partner

Canine Pointed tooth, one on each side of the jaw, used like a dagger

Carnassial Tooth located toward the back of the jaw that is adapted for tearing flesh

Detect Discover or find out

Distract To draw someone's attention away from something

Ensue To result from an earlier event

Evolve To develop gradually, sometimes over several millions of years

Fatal Causing death

Fierce Violent or savage

Flexible Capable of being bent

Gnaw To chew

Grooming To clean oneself or another

Hyoid A U-shaped bone at the base of the tongue

Incisor Tooth at the front of the jaw used for cutting

Intruder Something that enters a territory without permission or invitation

Melanistic The condition in which an unusually high concentration of melanin occurs in the fur of an animal, making it appear dark

Menacing Dangerous or harmful

Mimic To imitate or copy another's action

Obstacle Something that obstructs or hinders

Predator One that hunts and kills animals for food

Pride A group or family of lions, including cubs

Recessive gene A gene that does not express its associated characteristic

Rely To depend

Reserves Sections of forestland set apart for wild animals to live in

Rosettes Ringlike spots on the body of animals such as jaguars and leopards

Serrated Having a notched edge, like a saw

Shear To cut

Slender Delicate and thin

Stalk To chase prey

Tactic A plan or procedure

Tapetum lucidum A layer in the eye mainly of nocturnal animals that reflects light, causing the eye to glow when light strikes it in the dark

Territorial To defend one's territory or area

Texture The quality of a surface, rough or smooth

Index